Totally Useless Skills™

101 GREAT PASTIMES
OF PRACTICALLY NO REDEEMING VALUE

Totally Useless Skills™

▼▼▼▼▼▼▼▼▼▼▼▼▼▼▼▼▼▼▼▼▼▼▼▼▼▼▼▼▼▼▼▼

RICK DAVIS

Illustrations by Gene A. Mater

Photographs by Philip Noury

A Perigee Book

. . . to Sisyphus

Perigee Books
are published by
The Putnam Publishing Group
200 Madison Avenue
New York, NY 10016

The name "Totally Useless Skills" is registered in the U.S. Patent
and Trademark Office, by Rick Davis.

Library of Congress Cataloging-in-Publication Data

Davis, Rick, date.
Totally useless skills : 101 great pastimes of practically no
redeeming value / Rick Davis ; illustrated by Gene A. Mater ; photos
by Philip Noury.
p. cm
Summary: Provides step-by-step instructions for tricks and stunts
such as spoon hanging, pencil tricks, odd finger snapping, and disappearing body parts.
ISBN 0-399-51707-3 (alk. paper)
1. Tricks—Juvenile literature.   2. Amusements—Juvenile
literature. [1. Tricks 2. Amusements.] I. Mater, Gene A., ill.
II. Noury, Philip, ill.   III. Title.
GV1548.D28   1991
793.8—dc20   91-22473 CIP AC

Cover design by Lisa Amoroso
Front cover photo © 1991 by Philip Noury

Printed in the United States of America
1 2 3 4 5 6 7 8 9 10

This book is printed on acid-free paper.

ACKNOWLEDGMENTS

To give credit where credit is due, I have made a distinction between "sources" and "creators." The "source" is the person from whom I learned a skill, but who did not necessarily invent the skill. The "creator" is the person who actually invented the skill.

Like folk songs, most of these skills have been passed down through generations. Consequently, the names of most creators have been lost. Also, because I learned several skills many years ago, I regrettably cannot remember the names of many sources.

No skill, the creator of which is positively known to me, has been included in this book without permission. The following people are, to the best of my knowledge, the creators of these skills:

Jim Donlon: The Disappearing Tongue, Facial Aerobics
Dianne Ward: Creepy Walk
Rick Davis: Figure-Eight Eye Crossing, Eye Switching, Hand Break (inspired by Lee Faulkner's fish illusion), Disappearing Neck, Alternate Fingers, Inchworm Hands, V Hands.

I wish to acknowledge and thank the following people (my sources) for teaching me these skills:

Jan Bjune: The Rose
Rob Bryan: Smile
Louise Bourne: Lizard Face
Hovey Burgess: Feather Balancing
Dick Cavett: Mysterious Pencil Lift
Alicia Dattner: Upside Down
Jackie Davis: Side-to-side Eye Crossing, The Straw Worm
Constance "Nana" Davis: Finger Splits
Marc Davis: Straw Popping
Nancy "Mom" Davis: Mom Hands, Charleston Knees
Avner Eisenberg: Dual Hand Finger Splits

Lee Faulkner: The Principle of Circle and Square
Ron Gerhmann: William Tell Snap
Peter Gould: Hanging Three Spoons on Face
Otto Griebling: Disappearing Thumb
Mike Perry: My Favorite Airplane
Darrell Revel: Spider Hands
Jim "Uncle Jimmy" Richards: Thumb Split
Andy Robinson: Anti-Gravity Spoon
Phil Van Truen: Roll Coin Across Fingers
Bill Vanaver: 4/4 Hambones

AND THANK YOU:

. . . for a whack on the side of the head, Dick Kleeman;
. . . for great editing, Judy Linden and Sharon Stahl;
. . . for all photos, Philip Noury;
. . . for supporting my career: Bill Ballantine, Irvin and Kenneth Feld, Dennis McGlaughlin and Genevieve Aichele of NH Theatre Project, Richard Smith of Cuzin

Richard Entertainment, Bob Higgins of Entertainment Package, Benny Reehl of New England New Vaudeville, Jeff Loseff, and Chris Clemens of Robert P. Walker Enterprises.

... for guidance: Mark Anthony, Bobby Kaye, Lee Faulkner, Randy Judkins, Wanda Alexander, David Neufeld, Karen Lundh, Susan Jonas, and Jeffrey Gage.

... for modeling: Marcie Lightwood and Peter Berkrot.

... and Jackie, for everything. All my love.

CONTENTS

INTRODUCTION

▲

▼▼▼▼▼▼▼▼▼▼▼▼▼▼▼▼▼▼▼▼▼▼▼▼▼▼▼▼▼▼▼▼▼▼

You're eight years old. It's Christmas. You've just received a lot of presents. Some are useful, like socks, mittens, and sweaters. And some are not so useful, like toys and games. Now, I ask you, which presents do you like the best?

Or say you're forty. Some things in your life are essential, like a job, a home, and aspirin. And some things might not be absolutely essential, like flowers, laughter, and field hockey. Technically, you *could* exist without these things. But consider life without your home team, a good belly laugh, roses, or Aretha Franklin. These don't *ensure* our survival, but they sure *enhance* it.

And what is the purpose of ensuring life if not to enhance it? It's not enough just to exist; we must explore our potential. In this light, the non-essential becomes essential.

This is why I teach useless skills. They have a value, albeit a non-practical one. To say a skill is useless does *not* mean it's worthless. While essential things help us stay alive, non-essential things make us *feel* alive. The former allow life to merely continue: The latter allow it to flourish.

So what is a totally useless skill? It's any skill that entertains, enlightens, and contributes nothing of practical value to society. Notice I did not say "nothing of value"; I said "nothing of **practical** value." In fact, you'll find the skills in this book have great value. They will hone coordination, develop concentration, increase social interaction, and cure warts.

This all sounds well and good, but I confess: The only reason I call these skills useless is that if I called them totally **useful** skills, no one would buy the book.

I feel well qualified to teach because I have a degree in Philosophy . . .

. . . my first useless skill.

Obviously, since you've chosen to read a book about uselessness, you are a person of high intellect and refined taste. But, as you try some of these skills, at times you'll feel as coordinated as a drunk slug. As a result, you may mutter, "I can't do that," and give up even before you try. Our fear of failure is so strong that we would rather not even attempt a skill than risk looking bad. We all want to be instant successes.

While I can't guarantee that you'll be an instant success, with a little persistence you'll find the skills to be easier than you think. In fact, most of these skills can be mastered in the same time it takes to watch a round of television commercials. So (teachers and parents take note), learning useless skills will teach that you *can* do something special, if you try.

In addition, Totally Useless Skills are safe, non-addicting, and non-competitive. And, most importantly, they give me a good excuse to avoid gainful employment.

So, with this book I invite you to take your never-ending search for the meaning of life and give it a vacation. Put your brain on PAUSE, and come with me, boldly, where no curriculum has gone before.

READER'S NOTE:

▲

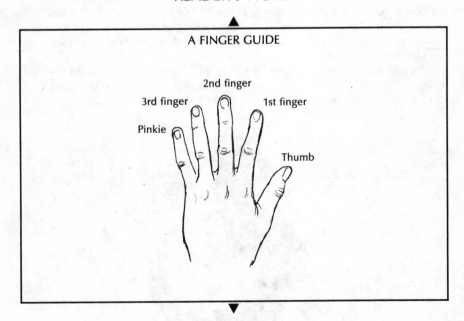

A FINGER GUIDE

2nd finger

3rd finger · 1st finger

Pinkie

Thumb

▼

I. DISAPPEARING BODY PARTS

1 ▶ THE DISAPPEARING TONGUE

1. Open your mouth. Stick out your tongue.

2. Cover your mouth with your hand as if to grab your tongue. Under cover of your hand, pull your tongue way back inside.

3. Keep your mouth open and take your hand away, in a fist.

4. Now, to put it back in: Put your hand back to your mouth.

5. Under cover of your hand, stick your tongue back out. Move your hand away, revealing the "restored" tongue.

Try this on your dentist.

2 ▶ THE DISAPPEARING THUMB

1. Thumb up.

2. Grab it.

3. Pull it off. Scream.

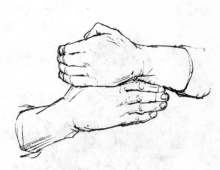

4. Put it back on.

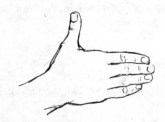

5. Does anyone need an explanation?

3 ▶ THE DISAPPEARING LEG

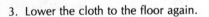

1. Cover your legs with a large cloth. Slip out of one shoe.

2. Bend your shoeless leg. (Duh!) Lift the cloth to just below knee level.

3. Lower the cloth to the floor again.

4. Slip back into your shoe, without the shoe moving.

5. With your best toreador impersonation, fling the cloth aside to reveal the "restored" leg.

4 ▶ THE DISAPPEARING NECK

1. Hold a cloth in front of you.

2. Raise the cloth. Scrunch your shoulders.

3. Lower the cloth. Hear gasps from your audience.

4. To bring your neck back, raise the cloth. Un-scrunch.

5. Lower the cloth to reveal your restored neck.

And for your next act . . .

II. BODY TRICKS

▼▼▼▼▼▼▼▼▼▼▼▼▼▼▼▼▼▼▼▼▼▼▼▼▼▼▼▼▼▼▼

5 ▶ ARM STRETCHING

Stretch both arms out in front of you. With one arm, make a large vertical circle, stretching it first down, then behind, then over the top, and finally back to the beginning.

It's a little longer now, isn't it? If you circle back the other way, your arm will come back to its original size.

6 ▶ ARM SHRINKING

Stretch both arms out in front of you.
Scratch the back of your head with one hand.
When you stretch that arm out in front again, it's a little bit shorter, isn't it?
Isn't it?

7 ▶ SKULL PENETRATION

Place the tip of your finger at the opening of your ear. (Not *in* your ear, OK? This is only an illusion.)

Stick your tongue into your cheek on the opposite side.

Keeping your finger at your ear, point it "up and down" while simultaneously moving your tongue "down and up" against the inside of your cheek. When the finger points up, the tongue points down, and vice versa.

. . . In one ear and out the other, right?

8 ▶ EYE SWITCHING

1. Pretend to pull your eyes out.　　　　2. Switch them.

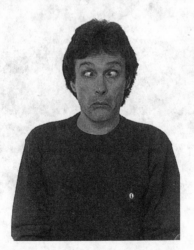

3. When you open your eyes, have them crossed.

Now switch them back before anyone realizes you're trying (and I do mean *trying*) to be funny.

9 ▶ NOSE BREAKING

You cannot graduate from kid-dom without learning this.

With your hands as shown, move them from side to side. At the same time click your thumb nail on the back edge of your front teeth. It will sound like your nose is breaking. You'll also notice your friends are groaning.

10 ▶ THUMB SPLIT

Place your thumbs like this:

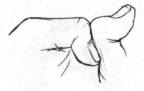

Place your right 1st finger over the gap between your thumbs. Now you can do this . . .

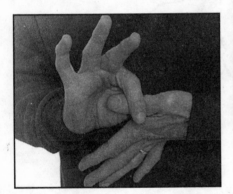 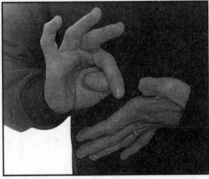

. . . and give your friends a coronary attack.

11 ▶ HAND BREAK

1. Face slightly to one side. Right palm is already resting on back of right hip, out of sight. Keep right elbow out of sight, too.

2. Now slide left hand behind back, and extend right hand into view. Time this sneaky action to give the appearance of one continuous motion.

3. Leaving the right hand where it is, bend your left hand back at the wrist, and swing your left arm briefly into view.

4. Swing your left arm back to the position as in illustration above.

5. Sneak your right hand behind your back; then, with perfect timing, reveal your left arm with its "restored" hand.

The effect will look like this:

12 ▶ CHARLESTON KNEES

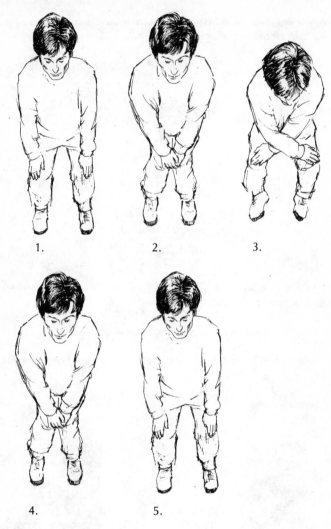

1.   2.   3.

4.   5.

. . . and repeat.

The three keys to this illusion:

1. Don't stop your hands in the middle. Make one continuous movement.

2. Alternate top hands.

3. Be willing to make a fool of yourself in public.

13 ▶ FINGER STRETCHING

Point out to a friend that your pinkie is shorter than your 1st finger.

Now announce that you can s-t-r-e-t-c-h your pinkie so that it is *equal* in length to your 1st finger.

Grab your pinkie and pretend to pull it. Secretly, tilt all four fingers to one side:

Your fingers should bend to the *side*, not forward. If your fingers don't bend this way, then try tilting your whole hand to the side, bending at the wrist.

Holding your fingers in this position, turn your hand so that the fingers point straight up.

When you display your hand, you'll see that now the two fingers appear to be the same length. Before your friend catches on, "pull" your 1st finger so that it is "back" to its original length.

▲

THE MYTH OF BEING DOUBLE-JOINTED

There is no such thing as being "double-jointed." People do not have two joints instead of one. The correct medical term is "hyperflexibility."

▼

And now for the moment none of you have been waiting for . . .

III. WEIRD FEELINGS

14 ▶ PALM POWER

Rub your hands together until they are warm. Now keep rubbing them until they are hot. Keep it up. Faster. When your hands are so hot you can hardly stand it, hold them like this:

. . . and you will feel an odd tingling between your fingers. Now spread your arms out wider and wider, pulsating as you go (as if you were playing a gradually enlarging accordion). The tingling will feel bigger and bigger. THIS IS A *WEIRD* FEELING!

Now *slowly* draw your hands toward each other until they are only an inch apart. As your hands come closer and closer, the tingling feeling will get stronger and stronger.

15 ▶ TWO NOSES

Cross two fingers.
Place them at the tip of your nose like this:

Close your eyes.
Now lightly rub the tip of your nose with your crossed fingers.
It will feel like you have two noses.
Touch the tip of your tongue with your crossed fingers, and it will feel like two tongues.
It will also feel gross.

The explanation of this phenomenon lies in the phenomenal workings of our nervous system. The nerves that run down the inner sides of the 1st and 2nd fingers eventually join into one nerve, while the nerves that run down the outer sides remain separate and go to two separate locations in the brain. So when you cross your fingers and touch your nose, you fool your own brain. The outside finger surfaces touch your *one* nose, but they send *two* separate signals to the brain. The brain mistakenly interprets these two signals as coming from two separate objects.

16 ► HOT DOG

Hold your fingers at eye level, about 6 inches in front of you.

Do you see a hot dog between your fingers?

You don't? That means you're focusing on your fingers. Look *past* your fingers and focus on something far away. You also can try holding your fingers at various distances away from your face.

If you hold your fingers like this  you'll see a ball floating in space.

If you hold your fingers like this  you'll see a heart.

17 ▶ FLOATING ARMS

Stand in a doorway and press the backs of your hands against the frame.
Count to twenty while continuing to press.
When you walk away, you'll feel your arms floating up.

I advise you not to try this at an art auction.

18 ▶ GLASS BETWEEN HANDS

With your hands together like this . . .

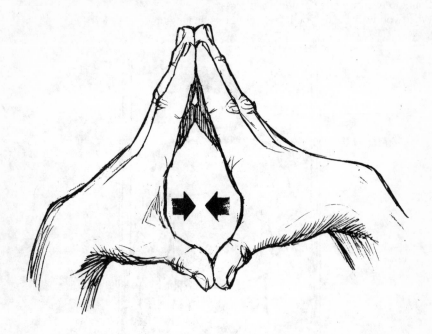

. . . pulsate your hands rapidly, keeping your fingers and thumbs together. Your palms should move about an inch toward each other, but not touch. (The ol' "spider doing pushups on a mirror," right?)

After about ten seconds, it will start to feel like there's a pane of glass between your fingers.

19 ▶ FINGERS TOGETHER

Have a friend clasp his hands and hold two fingers as wide apart as possible.

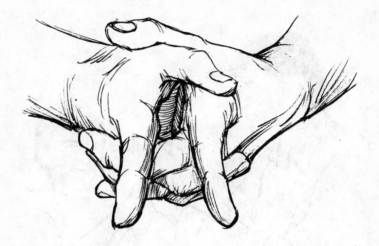

With *your* finger, rapidly trace a circle around your friend's fingers. Keep tracing this circle over and over. Mysteriously, your friend's fingers will slowly come together.

Your friend's fingers would come together anyway because the muscles fatigue eventually. But your circling action does serve as a mild form of auto-suggestion.

20 ▶ DEAD FINGER

Both you and a friend hold hands and point your 1st fingers up. Using your other thumb and 1st finger, rub the two upright fingers.

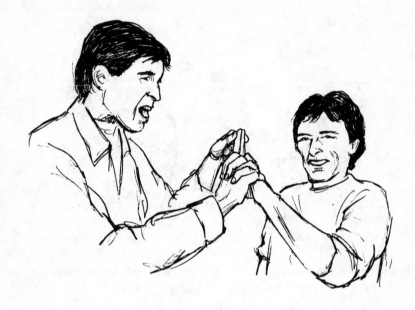

. . . it will feel like a dead finger.

21 ▶ MAGNETIC PENCILS

Press two pencil erasers together. Count to twenty.

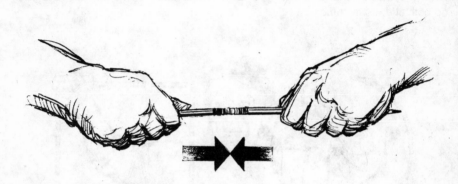

When you try to slowly move them away from each other, they will feel for a moment as if they were magnetized or stuck together.

WARNING: At the end of this sentence you may experience an unexplainable urge to turn the page.

IV. BOGGLERS

▼▼▼▼▼▼▼▼▼▼▼▼▼▼▼▼▼▼▼▼▼▼▼▼▼▼▼▼▼

22 ▶ CIRCLE AND SQUARE

Draw a circle in the air with one hand. Draw a square in the air with the other. Now do both at the same time.

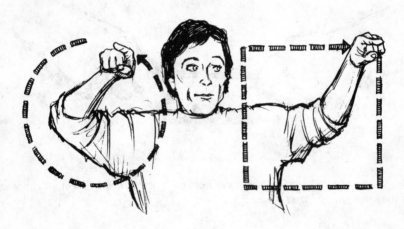

HINTS:

* Start by drawing just the circle.
* Concentrate your entire brain power (whatever is left) on the square.
* Draw one circle for every side of the square.

23 ▶ OPPOSITE DIRECTIONS

Trace a large circle in the air with one hand.
With the other hand, trace a smaller circle, inside the first circle, *in the opposite direction.*

Try twirling your thumbs in opposite directions. Same pointless idea. (Come to think of it, all circles are pointless, aren't they?)

24 ▶ UP-SIDE-DOWN

Your right arm goes . . . UP, DOWN, UP, DOWN, UP, DOWN . . .

Your left arm goes . . . UP—SIDE—DOWN—UP—SIDE—DOWN.

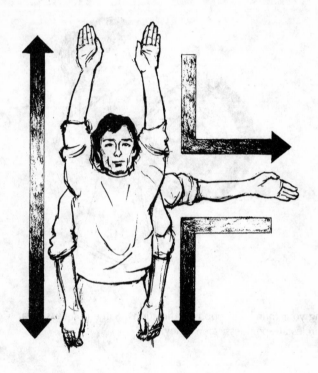

Now do both at the same time. And repeat.

Great for flagging taxis.

25 ► SIGN-CIRCLE

Try writing your signature while simultaneously tracing a circle on the floor with your foot.

26 ► OTHER NOSE

1. Hit your knees.

2. Grab your nose with your right hand, and your right ear with your left hand.

3. Hit your knees again.

4. Grab your nose with your left hand, and your left ear with your right hand. OK, got it?

2.

4.

Now repeat that sequence as fast as you can, until your cat starts looking for a new owner.

V. CHALLENGES

27 ► HANDS ON HEAD

OK, guys . . . think you're strong? Try pulling a lady's hand off of her head. You won't be able to do it.

THE RULES: Use one hand *only*. No pulling to the side; you must lift straight up. No jerking.

You can't do it because she's using her biceps muscle and you are using your triceps muscle, and her biceps muscle is stronger than your triceps.

28 ▶ PULL HANDS APART

The same principle (biceps beats triceps) is involved in this skill.

Have your friend hold her hands close to her chest, fingers pointing toward each other, elbows pointing to the side (not to the back).

Hold on to her wrists, and try to separate her hands by pulling to the sides. Betcha can't do it.

29 ▶ WALL LEAN

Stand with your left shoulder and the side of your left foot against a wall. Now try lifting the right foot without losing your balance.

Did you fall for it?

30 ▶ FINGERS OVER HEAD

While looking straight ahead, try to touch these two fingers . . .

. . . above your head on the first try.

Maybe the second or third try, but not the first.

Now, could I see your license and registration, please?

31 ▶ CAN'T-MEET PENCILS

Hold two pencils in front of you.

Here's the challenge: Try to touch the pencil tips together with one eye closed.

32 ▶ CHAIR PICKUP

1. Position yourself like this, with your head against the wall, four foot lengths from the wall.

2. Try lifting the chair and standing up.

You'll have no trouble at all doing this, *if you're a woman*. But if you're a man (sorry to tell you this) you won't be able to stand up.

Why? The reason is because women have smaller feet in relation to their height. At four relatively small steps away from the wall, women will have more of their upper body weight positioned over their center of gravity.

33 ▶ MOVE THIS FINGER

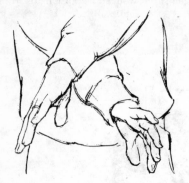

1. Cross your arms. Thumbs point down.

2. Grab your fingers.

3. Point your thumbs up.

Now, try to move the 3rd finger on the right hand *on the first try*.

▲

HOW TO MAKE "THE KNOT"
For the next two skills you'll need to know how to make something we'll call "The Knot":

1. Repeat Steps 1, 2, and 3 above.
2. Point your thumbs *forward*.

▼

34 ▶ SMILE

Make "The Knot" (see page 46).

Keeping your 1st fingers crossed, touch the right corner of your mouth with your right finger, and the left corner with your left finger.

NOW THE CHALLENGE:

Move from this position . . .   to this position . . .

without letting your fingers leave the corners of your mouth.

If you're all tangled up and can't move, don't despair; it *is* possible. Try it again using this new and improved way:

Cross your arms with the thumbs pointing down. Notice which hand crosses on top. If your left arm is on top of the right arm, make sure the left pinkie is on top of the right pinkie when you grab your fingers.

Now you can do it.

35 ▶ UNLOCKING FINGERS

1. Ask a friend to make "The Knot" (see page 46) with you.

2. Now challenge your friend to move to this position *without letting go* of his or her fingers:

THE SECRET: Sneakiness.

After you make "The Knot," lean over to your friend and say, "Let me see if you have that right." When your friend is not looking, secretly unlock your fingers and re-grab them as in View #2 above. Keep your fingers locked like this and turn your hands so that your thumbs point down.

Your friend, if he or she still is one, will not see the change. And it will appear the same as "The Knot."

You can now perform the above "One . . . Two . . . Three" motion with considerably less knuckle damage.

36 ▶ DOLLAR GRABBING

Starting position:

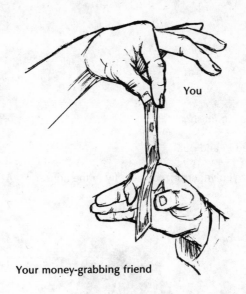

You

Your money-grabbing friend

If you drop the bill, your friend will not be able to catch it. Why? By the time the eyes alert the brain, and the brain alerts the fingers, and the fingers try to grab the bill, it's long gone!

And now, in case your fish are bored, may I present . . .

VI. GURNING (Funny Faces)

▼▼▼▼▼▼▼▼▼▼▼▼▼▼▼▼▼▼▼▼▼▼▼▼▼▼▼▼▼▼

37 ▶ LIZARD FACE

1. Frown.

2. Tendons stretched out.

3. Chin forward.

4. Eyes look up.
   And now for the big finish . . .

5. Flick your tongue in and out.

Repeat rapidly until you've terrorized every fly in the house.

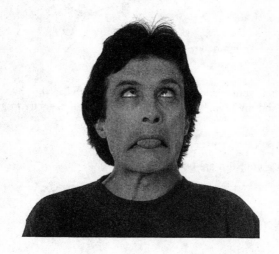

38 ▶ **FACIAL AEROBICS**

1. Start with your eyebrows up, and your mouth up.

2. Now keep your mouth up, but move your eyebrows down.

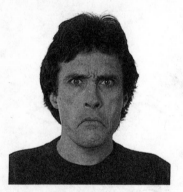

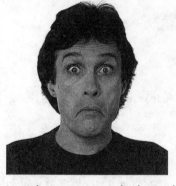

3. Now keep your eyebrows down, and move your mouth down.

4. Now keep your mouth down, but move your eyebrows up.

5. Now keep your eyebrows up, and move your mouth up. (As you did in Position 1.)

And repeat the sequence.

A lot.

In church.

39 ▶ ADVANCED EYE CROSSING I

Here's an interesting historical fact: The ancient Mayans actually thought of crossed eyes as a mark of beauty and would purposely train their eyes to be permanently crossed; yet somehow, modern anthropologists have not figured out why this civilization suddenly disappeared.

But don't be alarmed; my eye doctor assures me that a small amount of eye crossing will *not* make your eyes stick. It *will*, however, ruin your social life.

UP-AND-DOWN VARIATION

Most people look at the tip of their noses when they cross their eyes.

It's funnier if you look at the bridge of your nose.

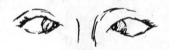

It's even sillier if you look at your forehead.

And now, for something truly demented, look at the tip of your nose, then up to your forehead, then back to the tip of your nose.

40 ▶ ADVANCED EYE CROSSING II

SIDE-TO-SIDE VARIATION

1. Point face forward and look to one side.

2. Cross your eyes . . .

3. . . . and look to the other side.

4. Now cross your eyes again and repeat the sequence.

5. Be sure to tell your psychiatrist you're doing this on purpose.

41 ▶ ADVANCED EYE CROSSING III

FIGURE-EIGHT VARIATION

This is similar to the Side-to-Side Variation, only this time, instead of following a straight line with your eyes, follow a sideways figure eight.

Start with your eyes crossed. Then look at the numbered positions in sequence.

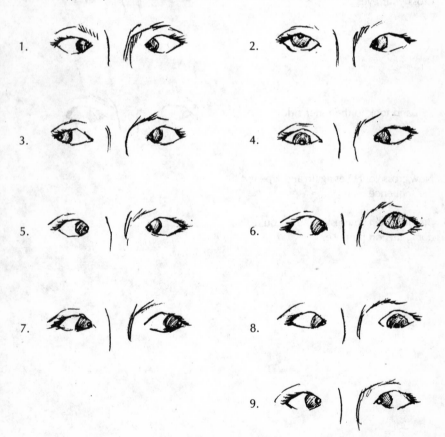

And now, how to impress people who are easily impressed . . .

VII. ODD FINGER SNAPPING

▼▼▼▼▼▼▼▼▼▼▼▼▼▼▼▼▼▼▼▼▼▼▼▼▼▼▼▼▼

42 ▶ THREE SNAP

You know how to snap one finger; now snap three in a row.

Snap 1, 2, 3 . . . FAST!

HINT: Use the sides of the fingers.

43 ▶ FLYING FINGERS

1. Hit a fist with your palm.   2. Switch. Hit your other fist with your
                                          other palm.

And continue.

Now for you more advanced types:

Do a three-finger snap (see page 55) with each hand before you hit.

44 ▶ WILLIAM TELL SNAP

Draw your thumb across your fingers in the direction of the arrow. As you do this, flick each finger forward.

Open your mouth and hit your cheek with these flicking fingers. Vary the shape of your mouth and you can play a decent William Tell Overture: To da' dump—To da' dump—To da' dump, dump, dump.

45 ▶ THUMB SNAP

Grab your thumb knuckle with your finger knuckles.
Squeeze. HARD!!
When you pull your thumb out, you'll hear a snap.
And in forty years you'll have arthritis.

46 ▶ CHIN SNAP

Make a "V" with your left fingers. Place your right 1st finger in the "V."

Put all these fingers under your chin. Find a fleshy part. Push up. Right finger starts to point downward, stretching the web of flesh between left fingers. Now sharply pull out your right finger.

You'll hear a pop.

HINTS:

• Push your fingers up hard. The goal is to create an airtight seal, so when your finger is pulled out a vacuum is formed. The popping is the sound of air rushing back inside the vacuum.
• Position the middle knuckle of your popping finger against your jawbone.

47 ▶ TOBACCO SNAP

Hold your fingers as in Position 1.

Raise your arm above your head, pointing your 1st finger up. Now, as if you were shaking a thermometer, sharply turn your wrist, and point your 1st finger down (as in Position 2).

1.

2.

As your 1st finger hits the side of your 3rd finger, you should hear a snap, or rather, a "wap."

HINTS:

* 1st finger must be extremely loose. Think spaghetti.
* Speed of the wrist rotation is crucial. The faster the better.
* Touching your thumb to the side of your 3rd finger might help. Experiment.

48 ▶ THE SOUND OF ONE HAND CLAPPING

Although it's a cosmic mystery that has eluded Buddhist monks for centuries, I can now reveal to you the secret behind the ultimate meaning of the universe: "The Sound of One Hand Clapping."

Start like this:

1.

2.

Wrist back. Fingers slightly curled and far forward. Pinkie farthest forward. Arm back. Point your fingers straight ahead, not at your head.

Starting from Position 1, with a whiplike action, throw your arm forward (Position 2) and immediately draw it back sharply.

You'll hear your fingers snapping, or rather, "slapping" against your palm.

HINTS:
* Wrist always stays back. Don't let it bend forward.
* Fingers must be extremely loose. Pretend they are not even there.

Great for drying hands, or accompanying mantras.

And now
THE AMAZING!
THE ASTOUNDING!!
THE NOT BAD . . .

VIII. PENCIL TRICKS

▼▼▼▼▼▼▼▼▼▼▼▼▼▼▼▼▼▼▼▼▼▼▼▼▼▼▼▼

49 ▶ MYSTERIOUS PENCIL LIFT

Try lifting a pencil exactly as shown.

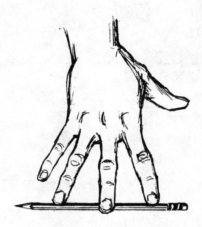

NOTE: The 1st and 3rd fingers are not *under* the pencil, but just touch the *side* of the pencil.

To do this, you'll need a pencil with ridges. Spread your fingers as wide as possible, then approach the pencil straight down. Jam the ridges of the pencil between the fingernail and the flesh of your 1st and 3rd fingers. Reach over as far as possible with your 2nd finger. Lift.

. . . Also known as creative pencil pushing.

50 ▶ THUMBS ON TOP, THUMBS ON BOTTOM

The challenge: Go from this . . .   . . . to this . . .

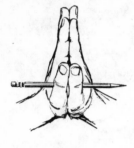
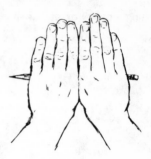

. . . and then back to this:

There's one RULE: You can't let go of the pencil.

Here's how it's done:
Start with the eraser on your left. Make an "X" with your thumbs, right over left. The fingers of the right hand reach between the thumb and fingers of the left hand. Right fingers hook around the eraser end. The left thumb hooks around the pencil near the point end. Right fingers pull eraser end to your right, and simultaneously, left thumb pulls the pencil point end to the left.

To reverse:
Again make an "X" with your thumbs. This time right under left, so that left thumb is between right thumb and pencil. Right fingers reach between left thumb and left fingers. Left thumb is under the eraser. Push eraser up with left thumb until you reach original position.

51 ▶ RUBBER PENCIL

A great classic illusion . . .

Thumb and 1st finger are held about one half inch apart. Pencil perpendicular to fingers.

IMPORTANT: *Your thumb and 1st finger never squeeze the pencil.* Relax that thumb and finger, hold them a half inch apart, and keep them in this position.

This trick is done with your arm, not your fingers. While keeping your fingers loose, move your whole arm rapidly up and down, rotating from the shoulder. Your arm will go up and down only a few inches.

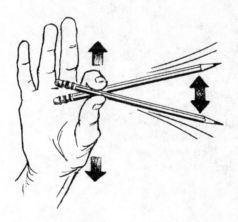

Voila! It's rubber!

If the pencil doesn't look rubberized at this point, you're probably: 1) holding the pencil too tightly, 2) using your fingers to vibrate it, or 3) not moving your arm fast enough.

The pencil appears to be rubber due to a phenomenon called "retinal persistence." Your ego appears to be enlarged due to a phenomenon called "instant talent."

52 ▶ FLOATING PENCIL

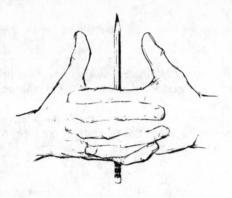

1. Fold your 3rd fingers down.

2. Grab the rest of your fingers, keeping your 3rd fingers back.

3. Hold the pencil top with your thumbs, and the pencil bottom with your 3rd fingers. Then let go with your thumbs, and show off your "floating" pencil.

53 ▶ SPLIT PENCIL

Hold a pencil at eye level:

Look at something far away.
Rub your palms together.
And the pencil will "split" in front of your eyes.

54 ▶ ROTATING PENCIL

1. Starting position.

2. 3rd finger and pinkie reach over pencil.

3. Release 1st finger.

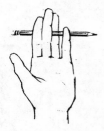

4. Pinkie reaches over pencil.

5. Release 1st and 2nd fingers.

6. 1st finger pulls up pencil from behind.

7. Release pinkie. You're now back to the start.

Learn this, and writer's block will never be the same.

IX. BALANCES

▲

▼▼▼▼▼▼▼▼▼▼▼▼▼▼▼▼▼▼▼▼▼▼▼▼▼▼▼▼▼▼▼▼▼▼▼

55 ▶ FEATHER BALANCING

Gravity is a real downer. If you try to balance something and it goes slightly off its center of balance, gravity will bring it down, unless you counteract gravity by shifting the center of balance. What does that mean? It means: If you want to balance, YA GOTTA MOVE! If you're balancing a broomstick on your hand and it starts to fall, ya gotta move your hand to compensate.

Balancing a peacock feather is easy because it is so light that air resistance will slow its fall. This gives you more time to adjust. Try it—you'll be surprised.

Now try it on your foot, elbow, knees . . .

Lean way back, look at the ceiling, and try it on your nose. Let it fall 45 degress, and then by slowly walking forward you can maintain the feather at this angle.

56 ▶ BALANCING THE BOOKS

Use an 8½ × 11 sheet of paper. Fold it like an accordion.
Folds must be *even*, about an inch apart.
Stand paper on edge.
Carefully lay book flat on top of paper.

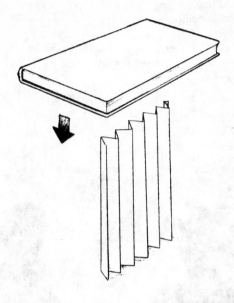

Each fold adds rigidity to the paper, allowing the book to be balanced on top.

57 ▶ PAPER BALANCING

See the line that runs diagonally from the top right corner of the paper to the bottom left corner? Fold paper along this line one inch from each corner. Leave the middle of the paper *unfolded*.

Place one corner on the tip of your finger. Raise your hand to chest level. Look at the top of the paper, not the bottom. Balance away!

58 ▶ BALANCE A QUARTER ON A DOLLAR BILL

Fold a dollar bill in half so it forms a "V." Stand it on edge on a table. Lay a quarter over the bottom point of the "V."

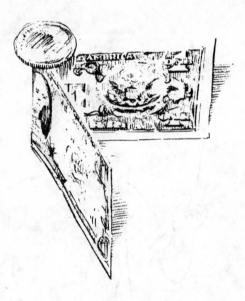

Grab the ends of the bill and slowly pull them apart so the bill becomes straight. The quarter will balance on the edge of the dollar bill.

59 ▶ GLASS BALANCING

With practice, a glass can be balanced on the edge of a plate.

Of course, a little help from your thumb makes this easier.

X. SPOONS

▼▼▼▼▼▼▼▼▼▼▼▼▼▼▼▼▼▼▼▼▼▼▼▼▼▼▼▼▼▼

60 ▶ SPOON HANGING

Never let it be said that you went through life without hanging a spoon on your face. This classic useless skill is guaranteed to attract the attention of any waiter or member of the opposite spoon-hanging sex.

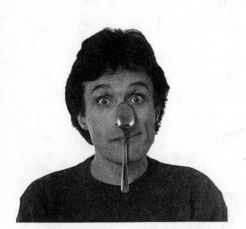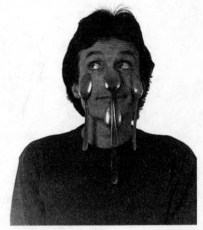

Clean a large spoon. Clean your nose. Breathe heavily on the spoon to make it warm and moist. Press inside curve of spoon hard against nose. Tilt head up slightly. Hold still, and let go.

If at first you don't succeed: Try rubbing the spoon vigorously with your thumb; or try bending the spoon slightly at the neck (otherwise known as "cheating"); or try different positions on your nose and different angles of your head.

VARIATIONS: Using the above method, try hanging spoons from your cheeks, your chin, your forehead, your forearm, your . . .

61 ▶ ANTI-GRAVITY SPOON

Press your thumb into a spoon, as shown.

Press down hard to make as much contact with the spoon as possible. This should also cause the back of the spoon to rise. Press the tip of your 1st finger against the end of the spoon, as shown. Slowly lift. Spoon appears to be magnetized to you.

Now do the dishes, will ya?

62 ▶ BALANCE A SPOON AND A FORK

Insert a spoon into a fork and a toothpick through the fork, and the whole contraption can balance on the rim of a glass.

Great for those slow-service restaurants.

63 ▶ SPOON PLAYING

Start by holding just one spoon like so:

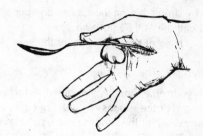

Thumb pushes down, causing end of spoon to push up against flesh at the base of the thumb. Think of the spoon as a seesaw. The 1st finger is the middle (or fulcrum). When the thumb pushes down, it causes the rear of the spoon to go up; but it's blocked by the fleshy mound at the base of your thumb. The result is a spoon that's going nowhere. It has a solid feeling to it. Go ahead, feel it.

The other spoon is held, upside down, between the 1st and 2nd fingers.

When you hold a spoon like this, you'll note it has a very loose feeling to it. Go ahead, feel it. In fact, it may want to "travel" side to side. So place your 2nd finger, 3rd finger, and pinkie lightly against the side of the spoon handle to prevent it from moving sideways.

Every hand is different, so experiment with different positions. Now pick up both spoons and prepare for major enlightenment.

Put both spoons in the same hand, back to back. Remember: TOP SPOON SOLID; BOTTOM SPOON LOOSE.

Rhythm #1: The OFF Position

Start by simply hitting the spoons on your leg eight times. Your empty hand is in what we'll call the "OFF" position.
Always bend at the elbow, never the wrist. Wrist is always straight.

Rhythm #2: The ON Position

Place your other hand, palm down, 6 inches over your leg. We'll call this the "ON" position. Hit the spoons on your leg eight times, exactly as before, only this time, on the upswing, hit the spoons on the palm of your other hand.

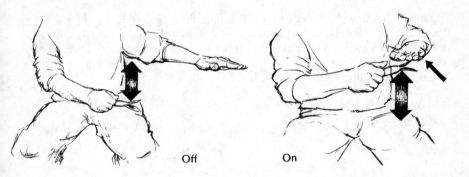

Off   On

IMPORTANT: The hand does NOT move to hit the spoons; the SPOONS move to hit the hand. Again, bend only at the elbow, never the wrist.

If you hit your leg 8 times, you should have heard 16 spoon clicks (8 leg hits, plus 8 hand hits). Now make 8 leg hits again, only this time, make 4 hits with your upper hand "ON" and 4 hits with your upper hand "OFF."

HINTS:

• Don't speed up when you put your hand "ON." Whether your hand is "ON" or "OFF," **use the exact same steady beat with the spoons.** Put your spoon hand on "automatic," and put your entire concentration on your non-spoon hand motions.
• When your hand is "ON," it's still. Let the spoons hit your hand, not your hand hit the spoons.

Got it? OK, try these rhythm patterns:

1) ON, ON, ON, ON, ON, ON, ON, ON . . .
2) ON, ON, ON, ON, OFF, OFF, OFF, OFF . . .
3) ON, ON, OFF, OFF, ON, ON, OFF, OFF . . .
4) ON, OFF, ON, OFF, ON, OFF, ON, OFF . . .
5) ON, ON, ON, OFF, ON, ON, ON, OFF . . .

Now mix it up, you hepcat.

Rhythm #3: Another Rhythm

1. Hold your hand as shown, slightly higher than your leg. Now you're going to make four spoon clicks. For Clicks #1 and #2, quickly draw the spoons across your palm and hit your leg.

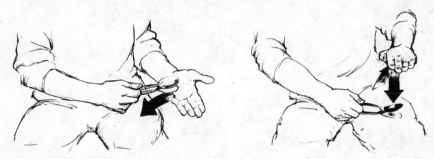

2. For Clicks #3 and #4, turn your hand over and produce two more clicks by first hitting your palm and then your leg.

3. Do all four hits, without any pauses. Start slowly at first, and build up to a fast speed. You're up to speed when you can do all four hits in one beat. It sounds like the drum in a military parade:

da da da DUM.
da da da DUM.
da da da DUMMMM DUMMMM DUMMMMMMMM.

You can produce some other interesting rhythms by first dragging the spoons across your outstretched fingers:

Drag the spoons across two, three, or four fingers, then hit your leg. What are these rhythms? I'll let you discover them yourself. It's more fun that way, and besides, you'll be developing your own style.

Now you know three basic rhythms. Mix them up. Switch from one rhythm to another, whatever way you feel. Make your own riffs, you creative genius, you.

64 ▶ FAKE SPOON BENDING

1. Go to Grandma's house for Thanksgiving dinner.

2. Hold her best silver spoon like this. Thumbs pointing up.

3. Rotate your hands so thumbs are pointing forward, as if bending the spoon. If you don't want Grandma to strangle you, study this illustration very carefully.

XI. STRAW TRICKS

▼▼▼▼▼▼▼▼▼▼▼▼▼▼▼▼▼▼▼▼▼▼▼▼▼▼▼▼▼▼▼

65 ► STRAW CLARINET

Squeeze the tip of a straw. Cut a small bit off each corner. Every inch or so, puncture small holes down the length of the straw.

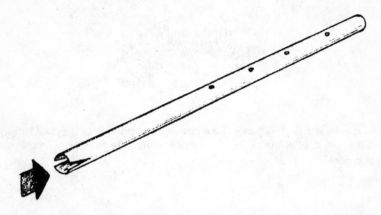

Hold your lips slightly apart and tightly against your teeth, then put the clipped end of the straw between your lips. With practice, you can buzz the straw and play it like a clarinet.

But you won't get to Carnegie Hall.

66 ▶ THE STRAW WORM

Hold a straw vertically and put one end on a tabletop. Then, push the paper wrapping from the top until it's all scrunched up at the bottom. The paper should resemble a concertina, or Wile E. Coyote after an unfortunate encounter with a rock.

Put a drop of water on this paper. (The straw is a good tool to use to do this.) The paper will weave and gyrate in the manner of a worm (after an unfortunate encounter with a fish hook).

67 ▶ STRAW POPPING

Hold a plastic straw like this:

Keep holding on to each end as shown, and rotate End A to the position of End B, and End B to the position of End A. Repeat this action several times until the straw looks like this:

Call over a friend and tell him you want to show him something incredible. When he doesn't come over, tell him you have free movie tickets. Now that you have his attention, ask him to flick his finger sharply at Point C. When he scratches his head and says, "I don't see any Point C," show him this book. Now, assuming he is still with you and he flicks his finger sharply at the middle of the straw, you will hear a loud POP.

Now give him the movie tickets, or get out of town.

68 ▶ BOTTLE PICKUP

THE CHALLENGE: Pick up a bottle with a straw, without touching the bottle with your fingers.

Here's how. You must use a bottle that has an opening that's smaller than its base. Bend the straw and stick one end in the bottle exactly as shown. You now can lift the bottle using the other end of the straw.

69 ▶ LONG STRAW

Make a tiny slit in the end of a plastic straw. The slit is about one quarter of an inch long and runs vertically down the straw from one end. You can now insert this straw into the end of another straw. Using the same method, you can link up as many straws as you think you can get away with.

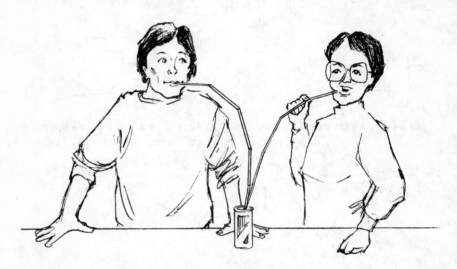

▼▼▼▼▼▼▼▼▼▼▼▼▼▼▼▼▼▼▼▼▼▼▼▼▼▼▼▼▼

70 ▶ THE BALLERINA

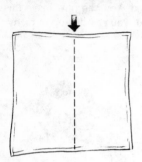

1. Fold a cloth napkin in half.

2. Tie a knot at the fold, then separate the corners as shown.

3. Grab the bottom corners. Spread your hands apart. Flip the napkin around as many times as you can.

4. Now bring the ends together, turn it over, and you have a lovely ballerina.

Release one "leg," and with a little help from your fingers, your ballerina will pirouette. If you release both legs and set her on the table, she'll do a split.

71 ▶ THE BUNNY

1. Put the middle of a cloth napkin over the back of your hand.

2. Put Corner A between the 1st and 2nd fingers. Squeeze. Now pull Corner A back toward you. Do the same with Corner B between your 3rd finger and your pinkie.

3. Push the flap marked X underneath your 2nd and 3rd fingers, and hold this mess of cloth with your thumb.

4. Pull the corner marked Y completely around your arm.

Bring Bunny to life by making a fist and moving your two middle fingers.

"What's up, Brain Surgeon?"

72 ▶ THE ROSE

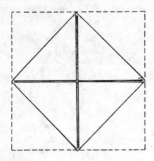

1. Fold all corners of a cloth napkin into the middle.

2. Fold all corners into the middle again.

3. Fold all corners into the middle a third time.

4. Carefully turn the napkin over without disturbing any of the folds. Now, from this side, fold all corners into the middle one last time.

5. Pinch the corners.

Turn over, and unfold the petals of your new rose.

If you're eating dinner with your wife and you suddenly realize you've forgotten her birthday, this napkin rose may actually save your life.

XIII. HAND GYMNASTICS

▼▼▼▼▼▼▼▼▼▼▼▼▼▼▼▼▼▼▼▼▼▼▼▼▼▼▼▼

73 ► MOM HANDS

I learned this skill from my mother when I was five years old, and since then I've never stopped learning useless skills. So beware, learning this skill could lead to the harder stuff.

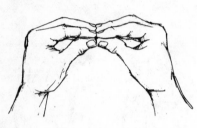

1.

2.

3.

4.

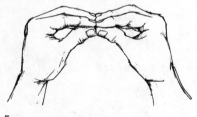

5.

6.

Repeat the sequence.

74 ▶ HAND TWO-STEP

Get married.
Put a ring on your left hand.
Place your left hand (with ring) on top of your right.

Now follow this sequence:

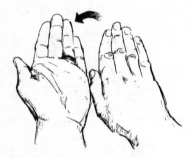

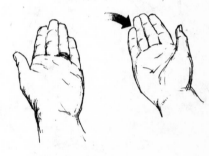

1. Open left hand.   2. Open right hand.

3. Close left hand.   4. Close right hand.

Keep hands in contact with the table.

You can now make the brilliant observation that your left hand (still with the ring) is on bottom.

Now repeat the sequence *starting this time with your right hand* (the one without the ring). Open, open, close, close . . . and now the ring is back on top.

Do this forcefully and you'll hear a sound. Do this quickly and you'll hear a rhythm. Do this repeatedly and you'll be hearing from your spouse's attorney.

75 ▶ FINGER SPLITS

Follow this sequence:

1.

2.

This can be done in two ways: by bringing all four fingers together between Positions 1 and 2; or by just moving the middle fingers.

Here's another, similar variation:

Starting with your right pinkie (palm down), move your fingers one at a time to the right. Then starting with your 1st finger, move them one at a time to the left.

76 ▶ ALTERNATE FINGERS

In American Sign Language, the sign for
"I Love You" is: Well, I've created a *new* sign . . .

"I love you not."

You'll notice that all the fingers have been reversed. Those that were up are now folded down; those that were down are now pointing up.* Try reversing the fingers repeatedly and rapidly in this fashion. "I love you, I love you not, I love you . . . "

Now try reversing these fingers: For a real toughie, reverse these fingers.

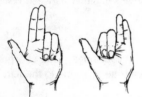

And for the truly insane, fold your fingers like this (look carefully) and reverse all eight at the same time.

HINT: Reverse one hand first, then, a microsecond later, reverse the other. If you do this fast enough, it will appear that you reversed them simultaneously.

*You'll also notice this sign is used absolutely nowhere.

77 ▶ CREEPY WALK

Place these two fingers on the tabletop.   Now "walk" these two fingers forward.

Et cetera . . . et cetera.

78 ▶ THIS SIDE—THAT SIDE

Touch your 1st finger to your pinkie, on top.

Then touch your 1st finger to your pinkie, on bottom. And repeat.

 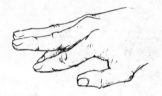

Like wiggling ears, this is one of those things that Nature has decreed some people can do, and some people can't. It has nothing to do with talent, but everything to do with useless genetic makeup. So if you can't do it, don't be depressed. If you can, don't be smug.

OK, try touching the 1st and 3rd fingers on top and on bottom . . .

. . . and the 2nd finger and pinkie, top and bottom.

All right, now try this:

1st and 3rd fingers touch on top, while simultaneously 2nd finger and pinkie touch on bottom. And reverse.

79 ► LOUD CLAPPING

Slightly cup your left hand, leaving a
shallow depression in your palm.

Clap your hands by hitting the right-hand fingers over your left palm. Hold your right-
hand fingers tightly together. You're going for an airtight seal around your left palm
except for a small opening near your left thumb.

Hold this small opening near your open mouth. As you clap, air is forced through the
opening between your hands and it echoes inside your mouth. It's louder than your
average clap.

Teach this to your mother before your next piano recital.

80 ▶ FINGER WIG WAG

Palms together, fold your 2nd fingers down.

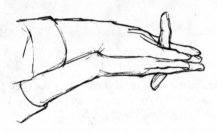

    Rotate your right hand counterclockwise and your left hand clockwise.* Make sure to keep right fingers on top of left fingers.

    Now do the "Wig Wag" by pointing the right finger left, and the left finger right; then the right finger right, and the left finger left.

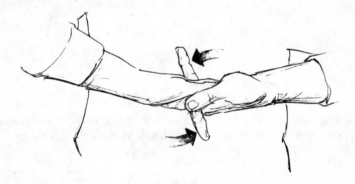

Given the fact that zillions of people have learned this before you, I think it's safe to say, "Congratulations, you've just joined the human race."

*Do the opposite if you're south of the equator.

81 ▶ HAMBONES

Three-Four Time
Hold your left hand, palm down, about 9 inches over your right thigh. Hold this left hand still.

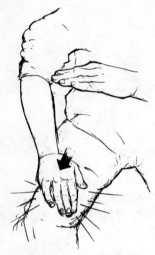

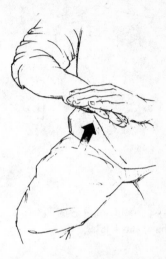

1. Right hand hits your right leg.

2. Right hand comes up so that backs of fingers hit left palm.

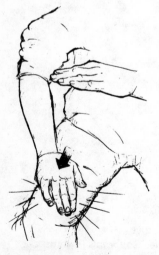

3. Right hand then hits right leg again.

When you do this, say "One, Two, Three" out loud. Remember, for now *only* the right hand moves.
Now let's go to the left side.

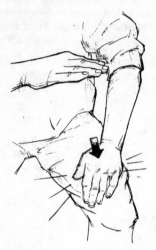

4. Hold right hand over left leg. Left hand hits left leg.

5. Left hand comes up to hit right palm, then . . .

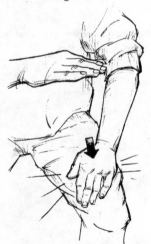

6. . . . hits left leg again.

Say "Four, Five, Six" out loud. Only the left hand moves.
Now repeat these six hits over and over, side to side. Go for this rhythm:

ONE . . . two . . . three . . . FOUR . . . five . . . six . . . ONE . . . two . . .
three . . . FOUR . . . five . . . six.

Always hit a leg on the downbeat. It might help you to count like a waltz (1, 2, 3, 1, 2, 3 . . .):

LEG, hand, leg, LEG, hand, leg, LEG, hand, leg, LEG, hand, leg . . .

Four-Four Time

Say this:

"One and two and three and four and one and two and three and four"

Every time you say a number, hit your right leg with your right hand. Every time you say "and," hit your left leg.

Easy.
OK, now you're ready. You've got the rhythm.
Using the same rhythm, say this:

"LEG and HAND and LEG and CHEST and LEG and HAND and LEG and CHEST"

When you say LEG, right hand hits right leg.
When you say HAND, right hand hits back of left hand. (The left hand will be positioned about 9 inches above your lap).
When you say CHEST, right hand hits chest.

Don't forget: Every time you say "and," the left hand hits the left leg.

HINTS:

♦ THE LETTER L. The right hand makes the shape of a capital letter "L" as it goes from leg to hand to leg to chest.
♦ Slow! Go slooooowly at first. If you always try it fast, you'll never get it.
♦ Speak the phrase "LEG and HAND and LEG and CHEST . . ." at the same time you make your hits.
♦ Now that you have the basic motion, try these variations with your right hand:

1) LEG and HAND and LEG and HAND and LEG and HAND and LEG and CHEST and . . .
2) LEG and HAND and LEG and HAND and LEG and CHEST and LEG and CHEST and . . .
3) LEG and HAND and LEG and CHEST*
LEG and HAND and LEG and CHEST*
LEG and HAND and LEG and HAND and LEG and HAND and LEG and CHEST.
*Pause.

82 ▶ INCHWORM HANDS

Follow this sequence:

1. Pray.

2. Bring heel of right hand to the finger-tips while keeping fingertips together.

3. Point right fingers up, while *simultaneously* moving left heel to meet right heel.

4. Go back and pray.

Repeat Step 2 starting with the left hand. Continue as before.

83 ▶ V HANDS

1. Start like this.

2. Right over left.

3. Right under left.

4. Right over left.

5. Right under left.

6. Right over left.

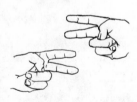

7. Right under left. Repeat, starting with
   Step 2.

84 ▶ SPIDER HANDS

Remember "itsy-bitsy spider"? (Left thumb to right 1st finger, then right thumb to left 1st finger, and so forth). Here's an advanced method. You'll be doing the same thing, only this time adding the 2nd and 3rd fingers.

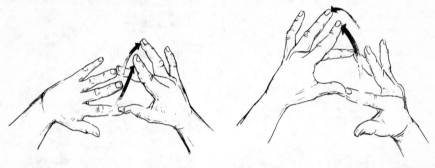

1. Right thumb to left 1st finger. Right 2nd finger to left 3rd finger.

2. Left thumb to right 1st finger. Left 2nd finger to right 3rd finger . . . and repeat.

HELPFUL HINTS FOR THE CONFUSED:

* The pinkies are never used.
* When you release your fingers, *raise them up*.

You now have a not so itsy-bitsy spider.

85 | ▶ HOLE IN HAND

Look through a tube with your left eye. Hold your right hand against the tube about 9 inches away from your nose. Keep both eyes open.

. . . You'll see a hole in your hand!

XIV. DILEMMAS

▼▼▼▼▼▼▼▼▼▼▼▼▼▼▼▼▼▼▼▼▼▼▼▼▼▼▼▼▼▼

86 ▶ THE BOTTLE DILEMMA

Put a bottle on top of a dollar bill. Now, try to remove the bill without tipping the bottle, touching the bottle, or jerking the bill.

The answer:

Roll the bill.

87 ▶ THE QUARTER DILEMMA

On a piece of paper, cut out a hole the exact size of a nickel. Now try to put a quarter through this hole without tearing the paper.

To do this, put the quarter on top of the hole. Fold the paper in half lengthwise without creasing. Bring the corners toward each other and the quarter will drop through the hole.

88 ▶ THE DIME DILEMMA

Set up a glass, two nickels, and a dime as shown below. Now try to remove the dime without touching it or moving the glass.

This can only be done on a table with a tablecloth. *Scratch the tablecloth near the edge of the glass.* The dime will creep out.

XV. ALL-PURPOSE, NO-PURPOSE SKILLS

▼▼▼▼▼▼▼▼▼▼▼▼▼▼▼▼▼▼▼▼▼▼▼▼▼▼▼▼▼▼

89 ▶ ROLL COIN ACROSS FINGERS

1) Hold hand in a very loose fist. If using your right hand, your knuckles should point to the left. If using your left hand, your knuckles should point to the right. Your knuckles should be together with no gaps between. Tilt your hand so that your pinky is slightly lower than your 1st finger. Now squeeze a quarter between thumb and 1st finger.

2) Now slightly raise the knuckles of your 2nd finger and gently push the quarter up with your thumb. Because your hand is tilted, the quarter should flip over and come to rest leaning against the 2nd finger.

3) Now lower the knuckle of the 2nd finger while simultaneously raising the knuckle of the 3rd finger. The quarter should flip over and come to rest leaning against the 3rd finger. Now lower the knuckle of the 3rd finger while simultaneously raising the knuckle of your pinkie. The quarter flips over and comes to rest leaning against the pinkie.

4) Now place your thumb underneath and in between the pinkie and the 3rd finger.

5) Un-tilt your hand so that all knuckles are level to the floor. Slightly separate the pinky and 3rd finger knuckles. This allows the quarter to drop through the gap and onto the thumb (which brakes its fall).

6) Using the thumb, push the quarter flat against underside of knuckles. Continue to push the quarter back to the starting position (against the 1st finger knuckle).

Re-tilt the hand, and repeat the sequence.

90 ▶ THE LONGEST WORD IN THE ENGLISH LANGUAGE

No, it's not "Supercalifragilisticexpialidocious." That's a Mary Poppins word, not a dictionary word. And no, it's not "Antidisestablishmentarianism." This word was used over a hundred years ago to describe a political-religious movement in Ireland. It's never used today, and besides, it's only 28 letters long. The actual longest word in the English Language (in *Webster's Eighth Dictionary* and the *Random House College Dictionary*) is 45 letters long:

PNEUMONOULTRAMICROSCOPICSILICOVOLCANOCONIOSIS*

. . . a totally useless word, but one you can use to give your friends the impression you are actually intelligent.
What does it mean? It's a type of disease . . . that you get when you pronounce long words.
No, really, it's a lung disease caused by a rupture (*CONIOSIS*) of the lung (*PNEUMONO*) that miners get when they breathe *ULTRAMICROSCOPIC* particles of sand (*SILICO*n) as they dig through igneous (*VOLCANO*) rock.
Use it the next time you find yourself inside a volcano with a shovel.

I find the second longest word to be much more interesting:

FLOCCINAUCINIHILIPILIFICATION

At 29 letters long it just edges out "antidisestab——"(you know the rest) as the second longest word. It means deciding something is worthless.
   Hmmm . . . would have made a good title for this book.

By the way, the oddest word is the word "SHORT," which becomes "SHORTER" when you add letters.

*NOO mon oh UL tra MY cro SCOP ic SIL i co vol CA no CONE ee OH sis

91 ▶ HEAD THROUGH A BUSINESS CARD

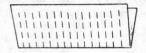

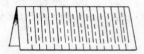

1. Fold a card and cut as shown. Don't cut all the way through.

2. Turn it over and cut between the original cuts. Be sure to skip over the first and last original cuts.

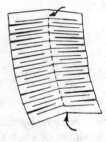

3. Unfold the card, and cut as shown. Notice that you don't cut the card at the top or the bottom.

Now spread it open, and stick your astounded head through it.

Using the same method you can: stick your body through a playing card; you and your friend through a regular-size piece of paper; or march a high school band through a poster.

92 ▶ THE MIME LEAN

First, get a feel of the position by giving yourself a dose of reality. Lean against a wall, for real, with your right hand. Lift your right foot, just for now.

Your arms and shoulders are now in perfect position. Now put your right foot down and gradually put your weight into it, but **hold the position of your arms and shoulders. Don't move them!**

This is the basic "lean" feeling.

Drop your left hip.
Put all your weight in the right leg.
Right knee turns inward.
Shoulder near ear.
Arm parallel to floor.
Fingers pointing straight up.

If you keep your legs, hips, and shoulders in the same position, you can do the following "leans" by just changing your arms:

. . . on a cane.

. . . on a mantle.

. . . on a shelf.

93 | ▶ HAT POPPING

Get a hat with a sturdy brim and hold it like this:

Your middle fingers are placed under the brim.

Practice flicking the hat as high as you can by flicking your fingers. Don't use your hands. Use just your fingers.

Now you can make it look like it is "popping" off your head.
Hold the hat high above your head.
Bring it straight down.
Just as it touches your head, flick your fingers hard so that the hat is launched.

HINTS:

- The illusion is enhanced if you continue to move your arms straight down, in one unbroken motion, until they are at your sides.
- When the hat pops off, don't look at it immediately. Wait a half second, then react.

94 ▶ YODELING

There are three types of people traditionally associated with yodeling: Swiss Alp dwellers, American Cowboys, and people who have stepped on broken glass. Usually thought of as a quaint vocal gimmick, yodeling was originally devised as an effective way to get rid of house guests.

But truthfully, you cannot yodel and be sad. It's a great shortcut to happiness. Here's how . . .

You first need to develop a "break" in your voice. This "break" occurs when you go from a legitimate voice to a falsetto voice (James Taylor to Mickey Mouse).

Do your best donkey sound. Go from a high pitch to a low pitch.

Now sing it. The "EE" sound is falsetto. (Falsetto sounds will be capitalized in bold type, regular voice sounds will be lower case.)

Now sing it backwards . . .

This is a "break" in your voice.

Now instead of singing "aw," sing "ay" (as in "day").

REMEMBER: "ay" is regular voice, "EE" is falsetto.

Sometimes, if you sing "ay" and then "EE," you'll notice the back of your tongue slightly rises. When yodeling, however, *the back of the tongue stays down.* You should feel the "EE" resonating lower in your throat. Be sure to keep your jaw absolutely still.

HINTS:

* Sing nasally, as in: "Naaa, Naaa, Na-Naaa, Naa."
* To find the break in your voice, S L I D E up from a low "ay" sound to a high, falsetto "EE" sound, with no silence between:

"aaaaaaaaaaaaEEEEEEEEEEEE"

- Take a deep breath before singing. Start singing "ay," and when you hit "EE" it may help to contract your abdominal muscles, forcing more air through your larynx.
- If you're still not getting it, start on a higher note. The "ay" sound should be somewhere in the top octave of your vocal range.
- On a musical scale, "EE" is usually sung six steps (or a "sixth") above whatever note on which you sing "ay." Don't know what a "sixth" is? Start singing "It Came Upon a Midnight Clear." The first two notes are a sixth.

For what comes next, here is a pronunciation guide:

> adle as in ladle
> lay-EE as in lady without the d
> odle as in yodel
> OO as in zoo

Now, don't sing "Little Ol' Lady Who." Instead, sing: "adle-lay-EE-HE."

adle - lay - EE - HE

*Sing these notes falsetto

In yodeling, the "ay" and "oh" sounds are sung in regular voice, and the "EE" and "OO" are sung falsetto. So, you can sing:

"adle-ay-EE-HE"
or "odle-low-OO-WHO"
or "adle-lay-EE-WHO"
or "odle-low-OO-HE"

Ready for some music? Try this little ditty:

O dle lay EE O dle lay EE o dle lay EE o dle lay EE O dle

1. lay EE O dle lay EE o dle lay EE OO DEE o dle

2. lay EE o dle lay EE o dle lay EEE!

For variation, now and then throw in an "adle" in place of an "odle."
For more fun, say the following, as fast as you can:

> Lottle-little-lodel-little-lay-EE,
> Lottle-little-lodel-little-lay-EE,
> Lottle-little-lodel-little-lay-EE, odle-lay

You can sing it like this: Sing "Lottle-little-lodel-little-lay" on the same pitch, any pitch. Sing "EE" six steps above that pitch in a falsetto voice.
Use it the next time you're attacked by a mad dog.

95 ▶ MY FAVORITE PAPER AIRPLANE

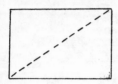 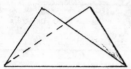 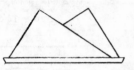

1. Fold a regular-size piece of paper along its diagonal.

2. Fold up one quarter inch from the bottom.

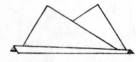

3. And fold again. Fold one edge slightly higher.

4. Use a table edge to smooth out paper edge.

5. Stick the thinner end into the wider end.

6. And fly away!

HINTS:

- Place 1st and 2nd fingers inside circle. Thumb on bottom.
- Gentle throw is better than hard.
- Heavier paper is better. Try a magazine cover.
- Make your plane's last flight into a recycling bin.

96 ▶ ANAGRAMS

This skill is for those of you who enjoy playing with words and letters. Both of you.

Words have many important uses. Without words, for example, we would have no way to write on bathroom walls. There would be no used car commercials, campaign slogans, or communication with parrots. Worse yet, we'd have nothing to do at dinner parties except listen to food being chewed.

But words can be useless, too. Despite all the words of philosophers, we *still* haven't discovered the meaning of life, the truth of our existence, or why the Cubs never win the pennant.

Some playful, but useless, variations of word play include:

PALINDROMES—sentences that are spelled the same forward and backward.
> *Top strategy: get art spot!*

CHARADES—sentences with the same letter order but different words.
> *Important: I do testing.*
> *Import antidote sting.*

And my favorite . . . ANAGRAMS. An anagram is a word or words that are made by switching around all the letters of another word.*

Some common anagrams are:

ADMIRER—MARRIED
THE ANSWER—WASN'T HERE
GOLD AND SILVER—GRAND OLD EVILS

and my favorite . . .

#*&%!(*)! — &!(*#)*!

Now, let's come up with a new name for you by making an anagram out of your current name.

Say your name is Dale Montague.* First, mix up all the consonants and write them on one line. Then mix up all the vowels and write them on the line below the consonants.

G D T L M N
A E U E A O

---

*Not to be confused with an ACRONYM, which is made from the first letters of a group of words. For example: MKS, (Manual for Correct Spelling).

*This name has been made up to protect the innocent. Myself.

I find it easier to spot new words when the letters are arranged in this fashion. When you see a new word (for example, the word "mule" in the sample above), cross out the letters and write down the word.

G D T L̸ M̸ N
A E U̸ E̸ A O
MULE

By continuing this process, I came up with "Go and eat mule." Another time, I tried "duel" as the first word, and I came up with "Mean goat duel." The possibilities, while not endless, *are* pointless.

HINTS:

* Letters like j, g, x, and z are used less frequently than other letters, so if these letters are in your name, use them first when making your anagram.
* If your anagram doesn't work out, go back and try a new first word. If it still doesn't work, go to court and change your name.

▲

THE TOP TEN ANAGRAMS OF THE NAME "DAVID LETTERMAN"

Tired TV lad name
Naive melted lard
A dim alter TV den
Ate a damn drivel
Deviled ant tram
TV Land admired E.T.
I'd vent lamed art
TV dream date? Nil.
A late DDT vermin

and   number   one...

Terminal Dead TV

▼

97 ▶ ONE-DOLLAR RING

1. Look at George and fold up the white margin at the bottom. Then, fold in half, and in half again.

2. End A folds up and behind.

3. Hold as shown and wrap End B around finger.

4. End A folds over and through the ring. A small portion then folds over the ring again.

5. End B folds over and tucks in.

If you did it right you'll see the number "1" on the front, and the word "One" on the back.

98 ▶ PADDLEBALL

For the benefit of those of you who have been frustrated by this toy (and I think we're talking "everyone" here), this is the secret to Paddleball:

Hit the ball hard. REAL HARD.
   Angle it 45 degrees.
   As the ball goes out, pull your arm back. As the ball comes back, quickly bring your arm forward again to meet the ball at the same original hitting position. The aim is for the ball to pull one end of the elastic, and your paddle to pull the other end, resulting in a "stretched-straight, no-slack" elastic.

The harder you hit it the better.
The longer the elastic the better.

I used to be a D.J., and I once achieved the unconfirmed world record for most paddleball hits on live radio. The unfortunate listeners were subjected to:

WAP . . . WAP . . . WAP . . . WAP . . . WAP . . . WAP . . . WAP . . . WAP . . . WAP . . .

Three thousand times.
This proved to be my last day in radio.

99 ▶ SNAP BAG

The Effect: An invisible ball seems to drop into a shopping bag.

The Method: Hold a shopping bag at the top edge between the thumb and 2nd finger. Throw up an imaginary ball. "Watch" it fall. Place the bag under the ball's "descent." Now, *snap* your fingers, and keep holding onto the bag. The sound of the snap and the motion of the bag will give the illusion that the ball has landed in the bag.

100 ▶ PALM READING

Believe it or not, there are some people who seriously believe the folds of skin on the palm actually mean something. But, being the enlightened, educated, and sophisticated person that you are, you couldn't possibly fall for those lines. Could you? That's why you're not reading this right now, right?

Let's face facts, reading palms is like eating fast food: Most people won't admit they like it, but they do. Regardless of what you believe, it's fun! Just follow these rules: 1) Say only good things, 2) don't predict the future, 3) say nothing specific, and 4) don't take anything seriously (especially this book).

▲

> Palm reading, or palmistry, is believed to have originated in ancient India and been "handed" down to the ancient Greeks, who probably changed it all around and passed it on to the Romans, who were so busy fighting wars that they gave their modified version to the rest of Europe. Then, in Victorian England, a man named Louis Hamon combined the sifted historical elements of palmistry with a little bit of imagination and business bamboozle to forge the basis of modern palm reading. Under the pseudonym "Cheiro," he was immensely popular at London society parties.

▼

Traditionally, if you are right-handed, your right hand indicates what kind of person you are *now*, while your left hand indicates what kind of person you *can* be. For lefties, vice versa.

There are three main lines:

The Life Line: The life line does not indicate the length of your life but, supposedly, its quality. If it's well-rounded, then you are said to be a well-rounded person. If it's a deep line, you are a deep person. If it's dirty . . . well, never mind.

The Mental Line: If you do not have a line here, you are in trouble. If your mental line intersects your life line, you are said to be a practical person who bases decisions more on facts than feelings, and vice versa if they do not intersect. If it angles downward, you are said to be a creative person. And just for your information, *everyone's* mental line angles downward.

The Love Line: The line you've all been waiting for. Is your love line curved? Then, supposedly, you are the kind of person who can give and receive love. AAAAAAHHHH. And just for your information, *everyone's* love line curves. If the right end of the line ends under the 1st finger, it's said that you are a giver in a relationship, i.e., you live partially or wholly *for* the other person. If it ends under the middle finger (if you'll excuse the expression), then you're a "taker" and you enter relationships only for your nasty, unscrupulous, hedonistic desires. (Lucky for us there isn't anyone with a line like that.) Most people fall somewhere in between, which is probably a healthy medium.

If all this is too much to remember, just remember . . .

THE ALL-PURPOSE, NEVER-FAILS, SURE-TO-PLEASE PALM READING:

"You are basically a happy person, although some things could be better. You have many strengths and you generally overcome your weaknesses. In spite of some negative thoughts you may have about yourself, there are people who love you. You will achieve success, but not in the way you thought you would. Good things will happen to you."

Works for anybody.

101 ▶ QUARTER SHOOTING

Make a face like a fish by sucking in your cheeks. Insert a quarter in the fold of one cheek. Now repeat after me:

PAAAAAAAAAAAAAAAAAAAAAAAAAAAAAAAAAAAAAAAAAH!!!!!!!!

. . . and the quarter will shoot out to the side.

Ten feet is the longest I've seen it done. Maybe, with practice, you can surpass this pinnacle of talent. In the meantime, have fun at your next tollbooth.

▲ ▲ ▲

Congratulations, you enlightened eccentric. By virtue of the authority (none) invested in me, I hereby confer upon you the degree of "Practitioner of Uselessness" (or P.U.).

The Institute of Totally Useless Skills

hereby confers on

_____

(fill in your name or make one up)

the degree of

P.U.

(PRACTITIONER OF USELESSNESS)

for needlessly mastering the following dubious talents:

—Advanced Eye Crossing
—Anagrams
—Balances
—Body Tricks
—Bogglers
—Disappearing Body Parts
—$1 Ring
—Paddleball
—Gurning (Funny Faces)
—Hambones
—Hand Gymnastics
—Hat Popping
—Head Through Business Card
—Mime Lean
—Napkin Puppets

—Odd Finger Snapping
—Palm Reading
—Paper Airplanes
—Pencil Tricks
—Quarter Shooting
—Roll Coin Across Fingers
—Snap Bag
—Spoon Playing
—Spoon Hanging
—Straw Tricks
—Weird Feelings
—Yodeling
—Pronouncing pneumonoultra-
  microscopicsilicovolcano-
  coniosis.

THIS USELESS DIPLOMA ENTITLES THE RECIPIENT TO ABSOLUTELY NOTHING, BUT DOES PROVIDE A USEFUL WAY TO WRAP FISH.

IN WITNESS THEREOF, THIS DOCUMENT HAS BEEN POINTLESSLY SIGNED BY A PERSON WITH VIRTUALLY NO AUTHORITY WHATSOEVER.

Rick Davis

_____

Master of Uselessness

The Institute of Totally Useless Skills
P.O. Box 1766
Dover, NH 03820

A BIBLIOGRAPHY OF USELESS BOOKS

▼▼▼▼▼▼▼▼▼▼▼▼▼▼▼▼▼▼▼▼▼▼▼▼▼▼▼▼▼▼

Beating the Odds in Las Vegas
Better Living Through Smoking
Scenic Vistas of New Jersey
The Sour Cream Diet
Life Fulfillment Through Daytime Television
Understanding Your Computer
Etiquette, by Charles Manson
In Search of the Loch Ness Monster
Fun in Nebraska
Picking the Right Presidential Candidate

Rick Davis, founder of the Institute of Totally Useless Skills, is a former Ringling Brothers Circus clown who has performed at DisneyWorld, on Broadway, on HBO, and in fifteen countries. He holds a degree in Philosophy (his first useless skill), and lives in New Hampshire with his wife and children, who tolerate his compulsive, expulsive, and repulsive singing.

Gene Mater works in his storefront studio in Bethlehem, Pennsylvania. He illustrates books and magazines, draws thousands of caricatures every year, and perfects additional useless skills. Here he demonstrates his version of the "floating pencil."